The Logician

Other books from EyeCorner Press
http://eyecornerpress.com/

NIGHT CAFÉ: THE AMOROUS NOTES OF A BARISTA
by GRAY KOCHHAR-LINDGREN
(philosophy, fiction, criticism, September 2010)

*COARCTATE: ANTIGONE'S RETURN
AND SELECTED POEMS*
by MARK DANIEL COHEN
(drama, poetry, criticism, August 2010)

PULVERIZING PORTRAITS
by CAMELIA ELIAS
(poetry criticism, January 2010)

JAGGED TIMELINE
by ROBERT GIBBONS
(poetry, bilingual ed. with an intro by B. Sørensen, December 2009)

*BETWEEN GAZES:
FEMINIST, QUEER, AND 'OTHER' FILMS*
by CAMELIA ELIAS
(criticism, March 2009)

*PASSION SPENT:
LOVE, IDENTITY, AND REASON IN E.A. POE*
by BENT SØRENSEN
(criticism, July 2008)

FEDERMAN FRENZY
by CAMELIA ELIAS, ed.
(criticism, October 2008)

FIVE FACES OF DERRIDA
by BENT SØRENSEN, ed.
(criticism, July 2008)

ÅRSTIDER I SKEPTIKERENS HIMMEL
by VALERIU BUTULESCU
(aforismer; udvalgt og oversat af C.Elias & B. Sørensen, July 2008)

THE
LOGICIAN

CAMELIA ELIAS

EYECORNER PRESS

© CAMELIA ELIAS | 2010

The Logician

Published by EYECORNER PRESS

October 2010

ISBN: 978-87-92633-03-3

© The author and EyeCorner Press 2010

Cover design and layout: Camelia Elias

The text has been typeset in Helvetica Neue

Printed in the US and UK

THE SUM OF ALL THINGS

ROSES for	**11**
.... The Mother	**25**
.... The Mathematician	**43**
.... The Prophet	**79**
.... The Fool	**109**

Acknowledgement

I thank all those who presently or absently have contributed to inspiring the thoughts, scenarios, and tableaus depicted in this book. Names are redundant.

For Ana

ROSES...

What's in a name? That which we call a rose
By any other name would smell as sweet.

— Romeo and Juliet (II, ii, 1-2)

At my mother's funeral in 1998 I had a moment of laughter. As the cask was lowered into the grave, the huge wreath made of red roses that was decorating the top slid off it, and down it went following the law of gravity, thus hitting the bottom. Everyone froze. The grave-diggers froze. They were having a dilemma. Should they continue with the cask, or shoud they dig out the flowers before the other job was done? Now, that was actually a very good question, and everyone could read on everyone else's face that the idea of having the flowers squashed was not a good idea. But then what? Who was to go into the grave and save the situation? No one was prepared for that.

I started laughing as all the alternatives seemed to have the potential of instituting a hillarious moment rather than one of mourning. One of the grave-diggers took advantage of the situation, and as he was still holding on to the cask he started lamenting: "you've got to believe me. I had no intention of doing this. I didn't do it intentionally." I started laughing even harder. My sister was pinching me to stop, but I couldn't. "Please, you've got to believe me," the poor man continued. And it was clear to me that until I said something, we were all going to remain frozen in time. So I said: "I believe you." "Really?" the man said. "Really," I said. This conviction brought about a smile on the poor man's face. Without further thinking about it, he started lowering the cask. Ok, I said to myself, so we do have a solution which beckons itself unto us, leaving us precisely in a state that some logicians call consequentialism—formed by the moral actions that create a structure for judgement. In other words, if you need to do something, it doesn't matter what way you choose in order to acheive that; you just do it. As many can relate to this approach, there is often no objection to the pragmatism which dictates that the end justifyies the means. I came out of my reverie when the sound of squashed flowers became a testimony to the fact that this very pragmatism was taking place. Along with the fact that everything passes. Bodies and morals alike.

I could hear mother laughing from the grave. "Logically speaking," she would say, "you cannot believe anything. But logically speaking, you can laugh without a reason. Because logically speaking, it is imagination that keeps you sane, not reason." Errr, yes, I seem to remember that there was a different type of coherence in mother's line of argument, but now I forget which. In any event, belief and methodology, for mother, always implied more than factual knowledge, though she did like going with the facts.

Now, why would mother laugh beyond the grave, I asked myself? Of course, I thought again, because she was a Marxist who believed in transcendence. "This is how we do things around here," she'd say, but we'll turn everything into a ritual because this way the tedious task of getting on with the program will not be so mechanical and boring. Now, that was sound logic to me. Although an inveterate Marxist, mother was thus a woman of rituals. I owe my bathroom rituals to her. When she decided to put a red Persian rug on the tiles, I decided to build shelves for books. The more the books piled up, the more decadent the bathroom looked. A cross between a brothel and a well stocked library. "Yes," mother would answer the phone when someone would call, "no, she's not available," she'd say. "She is in the lecture room — Yes, yes, the *salle de la lecture*," she'd insist.

I kept this ritual when I moved to Denmark, though the practice of changing the book categories according to subjects grew more sophisticated. Books about cosmology were paired with books about the theatre of the absurd, and so on. Only once did I change the shifting categories of books in the bathroom at the request of visiting guests. When they kept asking whether there was a reason why I had all the famous psychoanalysts in the bathroom and suggesting that their presence made them feel rather uncomfortable while relieving themselves, I replaced them with other ones. Now, especially on a holiday, I like the idea that if you don't go to church, the synagogue, or some other such place of worship, you go to the books, if you are a type of person who is interested in 'the word'.

Right now my bathroom is populated by all the favorite Jesuits, the Kabbalists, the interesting contemporary theologians, several bibles in several languages and editions, and other such ancient texts. You get the picture. My morning ritual begins with a good look in the mirror. Mother was adamant about the importance of this act, as it is done in a moment when the silence of the night still lingers on. You're awake, but you're still dreaming, and there's a good chance of catching a glimpse of yourself as a ghost. I'm getting there. These days it is my hair that fascinates me. Then, I let my eyes glide down over the spines of the books, and make an instant selection. Today it was Balthasar Gracián's *Oráculo manual y arte de prudencia* (1637) that caught my gaze. The word, oracle, made me think of my mother's other interest, and one which was nurtured with as much care as she did her Marxism. She liked going to the prophets in town. This was usually not an affair that one was loud about, and you had to know the right people if you wanted to get in touch with these saints. She used to make my sister and me swear that we would never disclose our exciting activity of visiting, which, however, often involved a bathetic conclusion: "By Jove," mother would say, "such nonsense, but how I love the passion in it."

Indeed, what the prophets had to say was nonsense, but the fascinating part was sensing that at least where mother was concerned she really would have liked to come across the truly astonishing part which would have placed her in a state of grace. So she was always hopeful. And it wouldn't have mattered which one, as long as it was there (the Catholic theologians distinguish, for instance, between actual grace and sanctifying grace, accidental grace (*gratia creata accidentalis*) and uncreated substantial grace (*gratia increata substantialis*), efficacious, sufficient, irresistible, infinite grace, and so on. You get the picture). But states of grace are hard to come by, and for the most part, what we are left with is making distinctions rather than experiencing them in their fullness of beauty and being. I read these lines from Gracián in the bathroom:

> Do not die of the fools' disease. The wise generally die after they have lost their reason, fools before they have found it. To die of the fools' disease is to die of too much thought. Some die because they think and feel too much, others live because they do not think and feel at all. The first are fools because they die of sorrow, the others because they do not. A fool is he that dies of too much knowledge. Thus some die because they are too know-

ing, others because they are not knowing enough. Yet though many die like fools, few die fools. (180)

Mother's life ended, but it occurred to me that if there is something that never ends, it is devising strategies for testing our courage when it comes to making distinctions between house oracles and heart oracles, especially when we know that revelations about their inner qualities rely on bells ringing. One such bell reverberates in my head, as we speak, through the words of Gertrude Stein, ringing through Alice B. Toklas, ringing perhaps for an upgraded spot in the bathroom: "I may say that only three times in my life have I met a genius and each time a bell within me rang and I was not mistaken." Augustine approves: *Ipsi sancti in ecclesia sunt alii aliis sanctiores, alii aliis meliores.* And Cioran is winking from the top shelf next to the shower. I pick that one up as well.

Mother could never understand why I like to read Cioran. "Sure, he's good," she used to say, "but isn't he over the top?" I remember that I disliked her comment. "So what if he's over the top, if indeed that is the case," I would retort and then remind her that particularly a woman like her should know better. And what kind of woman was she exactly, some might like to know. She was fascinating and awesome, and awe-inspiring. What fascinated me about her was her ability to combine total mercilessness with soft reason. She was brutal in her approach to facts, which she always formalized down to the "meremost minimum," to use a Beckettian phrase, as mother and Beckett had a lot in common. "This is this," she used to furthermore say, "not something else." "Sure," I would say, feeling crushed by *reality* "but listen to this," and then I would venture into some counter-argument that would make the matter-of-fact situation appear more nuanced — or so I liked to believe.

What I liked about mother was the fact that although she was always ready to bulldozer my exposition, she would often also go: "I see your point – beyond the fact" – which would stop her demolition project. As I grew older, I understood how what enabled her to be both uncompromising and yet flexibly reasonable about listening to how "this is this" might also be something else. She always hoped that people, even when living most inauthentic lives for the most part, had the potential to reveal their *religious* dimension within themselves and to her. Expecting this of everyone was a tall order, however, and it didn't make her popular. On that, one could then say that she was as over the top as Cioran, whom I still read for the exact same reason: that he really believed that reading for the soul, rather than the plot, is infinitely more interesting. We narrativize our existences all the time, all according to the variables which are available to us for permutation and which enable us to feel good about ourselves. But the soul, as mother and Cioran seem to suggest, has its own set of channels through which to manifest itself.

Through crystal glasses, for example. When mother talked about crystal glasses, I was in for a revelation in a class of its own. She had a thing for them. As a young girl, she had some. Then communism hit Romania. Her family lost not only land but also most of the crystal. From then on it went down the drain. By the time my sister and I came along in the late 60s, there was no more crystal in the house. She tried her best, but she didn't have the right connections. At some point, two of her nieces got their hands on some crystal, and mother got excited. One of the girls had a job in a department store, which was as close as one could imagine coming to the possibility of touching the damn thing. But in Ceausescu's Romania, every time there was a delivery, mother's name slipped from the crystal-list. "Where are my glasses?," she would ask my cousin. "Gone," she would say, "so quickly that I couldn't even get to the list under the counter." "Damn," mother would say. She ended up cursing the system and her hard-working niece. The system fell in the 90s and the niece got her glasses smashed when she moved to another place. Most of them. Mother felt avenged.

In any event, she used to think that most of the people she knew were made incurably stupid by the system. Including her nieces—when it came to valuing their possessions. The crystal, that is. Most of the crystal mother came close to used to be locked away safely in a display-window. The family always insisted on pulling a horrified face when mother would make the glasses vibrate with her fingers. "Careful, auntie, careful," they would cry. "They'll break." They would then hurry to fetch some ordinary glasses and make mother drink whatever liquids were available from them. Mother would get high blood-pressure, and it was up to my sister and me to rescue her from the world's stupid mentality, and from dying. I now have the best crystal glasses in the world. They are so beautiful and fantastically crafted that my sister and I literally forget to eat in their presence, in the face of listening to a whole symphony of sounds that make the whole house vibrate more than the bells of the biggest cathedral in the land. We always toast for mother, and we always imagine her turning in her grave. From pleasure, of course. I like to think that we make up for what she was missing. In the glasses.

This book celebrates the genius of my mother, who was a most formidable logician, and is an acknowledgement of her wit and formal thinking which have informed my whole creative endeavor. In this book of fragments and prose poems I hope to pass on not only her sense for numbers, but also her sense for love, higher grounds, and contemplative calculations beyond formalism. "In love and logic," she would also say, "the only strategy that works is the one that allows you to figure out just how smart you are." That's the logic of basic living.

Although only few fragments are dedicated to materializing more concretely through language and event how the figure of the mother emerges, they are, however, crucial, insofar as they are meant to manifest both implicitly and inherently what I imagine all mothers want to pass on to their children: namely, how to be grateful. How to be grateful especially for the moments in life and art that enable us to experience what Clive Bell called "the significant form." Experiencing form as significant enables our reflective capacity to relay what it means to come across beauty. How do we experience beauty, especially as it can stretch between a range of spaces, some vast, some sublime, and some grotesque? As others have also remarked, "beauty is difficult" (Aubrey Beardsley on his deathbed speaking to Yeats). Indeed it is.

I was fortunate enough to have a mother who, while often speaking with a forked tongue, made a lot of sense: "logically speaking, there is no problem. Morally speaking there is a problem," she'd say. For, logically speaking, the experience of the significant form—even as it relates to the realm of the somewhere in the unfinished or the *je-ne-sais-quoi* of a situation which leaves us crushed and in pain—must come from acknowledging that the necessary pain that goes into it, into trying to grasp that which resists full comprehension, is what gives shape to the transcendental potential. We may be left writhing in the dust, as it were, in our encounter with beauty, but it is precisely this pain that enables us to be grateful for what we experience. Morally speaking, there is thus a problem in terms of how we receive from others what we ultimately deem as singular, or unique experience. For, if the pain we normally associate with learning, knowing, or trying to grasp the ineffable or the unrepresentable is not properly understood, then, it will necessarily illicit not a grateful but a vengeful attitude. Here, one of the lessons that I attribute to mother's teachings is this one: as avenging subjects we lose sight of our own, otherwise noble, preoccupations when the desire to accede to what touches us closely escapes actualization. And that's bad.

Here mother would say: "you can elect to get back at the ones who try to teach you something beautiful, if you don't get it, but you can also try to make an effort and see what motivates their own effort, and where it comes from. But this takes time." In a way this book is about the time it takes to appreciate what and who inspires us in our lives. It is about distinguishing between preoccupations, desires, and beautiful experiences that make us think of what is important to value in life, namely, any authentic response to our inexpressible finitude.

My father died when I was eight. Mother never remarried. Not because she didn't want to, but because she didn't find anyone who could make her see things in a nuanced and different way than the one she was accustomed to. She inherited half of what was supposed to be my father's pension. As he was only thirty-nine when he died, this sum didn't amount to much. My sister and I were informed of the situation, and of the fact that this situation afforded us only two options on Sundays. Mother wanted democracy in her household, so for ten years or so, every Sunday she would pose this question: would you like to go for cake, at the fancy patisserie in town, or roses? We went for the roses most of the time.

My dear Ana, this one is to you. For all the roses. Even though, as you also put it: "logically speaking, there's no point to sentimentality, for we're all going to go mad and die sooner or later. Therefore, and precisely therefore we can keep on loving *ad infinitum.* It will make no difference or all the difference, in the end."

If I argue with this position, here, now, will you turn in your grave? — Dead Ana replies from the beyond: "if it's there, the love, it'll always be there. If not, there's no loss. But meanwhile, let's hear it first. Let's hear it."

Only what touches us closely preoccupies us.

We prepare in solitude to face it.

— Edmond Jabès

... FOR THE MOTHER

POLITICS OF SELF-DISCLOSURE

For prima logiciana

The rainbow over the top of the mountain leaves me with the feeling that my lips are red and lush. Sounds come out of my mouth, as I take in the green, the purple, and the black. The words are those of my dead mother: "it's not the end of the world that you can't figure out what two plus two is." I'm not good at counting. She was. This is her speaking as a mathematician. As the logician that she also was, she would say: "enlightenment while walking the path to the top is possible if and only if you wear good boots." As the physicist that she was too, she would say: "create atmosphere!" I read my lips in the lake. Oh, they are so beautiful! They are still red. But whose language do they speak?

I disclose myself to create a private language that is not my mother's. Self-disclosure creates private knowledge. I like the knowledge that a private language affords me: my mother only read one novel in her life. She liked it so much that she was convinced that another novel would ruin her first experience. Hence she never read another. She was a trained logician, did I say? I think the thoughts of the mountain. High on the plateau, I'm always sorry.

Morbidity grasps me and my mother is not there to save me. Philosophy does. Even though it's stupid. "Death is the only intellectual property we have exclusive rights to," I instruct myself. But in the strangeness of being, I cry.

SUITORS

For Ana and Georg

My mother was 40 when my father died. He was younger. She had suitors. One after one after one until I couldn't tell the difference between the analogies: was she Homer's or Joyce's Penelope? Mother was chaste, and wouldn't give in, but only because all the suitors were stupid, she thought. Homer's and Joyce's Penelope also thought that. Some of the suitors were rich. One in particular had a goddamned palace. He thought mother was beautiful. But mother was mainly as smart as a Rolex Perpetual. The Oyster kind: soft on the inside and rough on the outside. Sharp eyes. Rough in her speech. But her breasts, oh, so curvy and soft. She spoke with the precision of a split beam. "But we want you," the suitors would argue, often committing the *argumentum ad hominem* fallacy, when she would politely turn them down. The evening before such events, I was always asked to imagine whether I could see her washing the suitors' underwear. Ever. I never could, so that settled it.

Mother was a logician and would quickly get tired of uninteresting fallacies. "Give me a goddamn challenge" she would say, but the suitors never thought of arguing by way of making recourse to fashion strategies.

Every month the rate of suitors coming to woo would also have a down curve. That's when mother would make lamb roast in cardamom. She would serve a bran fermented drink, made all according to the secret recipe of her now vanished without a trace Yiddish speaking ancestors and serious people in the diamond business. Well, religion and badly applied communism can do marvels for turning traces into supplements. Mother became a Marxist thereafter, so she wouldn't have to worry about a thing in the world. But she still liked going to the prophets. When she would stop worshipping the senses of the mind, however, she would throw herself at worshipping food. With the lamb, there was always an announcement. A competition was open for the best argument to win. She would listen to the pros and cons as to whether changing the whole goddamn furniture in the house was a good idea. It always was, so we always changed it.

This went on between suitors coming and going while mother was busy counting how many stupid ones there remained who just couldn't see how smart she was. She kept counting between the age of 40 and 50. So, 12 times a year, 10 years in a row, the furniture would follow the suitors' suit: off it all went; off they all went. It was an interesting time, and the furniture got better and better. The suitors couldn't follow suit. I'm in my 40s now. I weigh 50 kilos. I read Lacan and syllogisms before bed. I also read other things before bed. But never in bed as such. In bed I'm naked. No books. Just thoughts. And heat. There isn't a lot of furniture in my house, but the little there is, is goddamn topnotch.

OLD MASTERS

For T.T.

Behind the curtain on Christmas Eve my mother's voice merges with Bishop's: *"The art of losing isn't hard to master / so many things seem filled with the intent / to be lost that their loss is no disaster."* Mother's voice is as soft as the softest rain: "Watch now, how men will lose their one chance to kiss the alabaster of my face." Widows and lesbian lovers *"Lose something every day. Accept the fluster / of lost door keys, the hour badly spent. / The art of losing isn't hard to master."* " — Is she at home or not," the horny men ask, but hers is not the task to answer to the charge of forgery and fidelity in life and in disaster. *"I lost two cities, lovely ones. And, vaster, / some realms I owned, two rivers, a continent. / I miss them, but it wasn't a disaster."*

The sounds get intense, and men's excitement turns into a disaster. "This is a disaster," they all shout. "Every year the same thing. It's Christmas for Christ's sake, indulge our lust, for once, and be a sport." But "No," she says, with Echo as her partner, practicing the art of losing even faster, one art which I am made to see as she refers once more to some disaster: " — *Even losing you (the joking voice, a gesture / I love) I shan't have lied. It's evident / the art of losing's not too hard to master / though it may look like (Write it!) a disaster."* "I'm listening," I say, "But if it is as if it looks like it, like a disaster, then why do I have to write it, when those intended for, this writing of disaster, go back to eating, or opening their windows, disgruntled so by their fail to muster, or is it master, you?" "— Don't move," I say, "I'm painting you as implacable. Me, as lightness of touch on your lips, so that the one you're waiting for will come at last. At last."

THISNESS

For the Russian reader

What love knows is always thisness. *Haecceitas*. Dialogue is necessary but only on a gliding surface. The quiddity of whatness. My Russian speaking mother knew the distinction between reading and reading the other. The other of the other. The author has been dead for a while, and then resurrected. Now the other is both. "You are the master," she said. "You know what love knows." I bowed. She was a grand This. We all love our mothers, no matter What. The quiddity of matter is the haecceity of soul. Descartes got a good spanking from the Madonna, our Lady of the Spirit, and became an accidental tourist. Losing his head like that! Ahhh, being this woman! What bliss! Hylomorphism is a piece of cake in her mouth.

ZWECK

For Grigori Perelman

The 32 diamonds in my ears sparkle against my mother's greeting: *Bonjour tristesse!* Diamonds have *zweck*, she says, and then she urges me to drop speaking in boundary sentences. They can be false as well as true. She tells me why her logic is the Janus faced science of mathematics. I respond to her greeting with this one: *von hier bis unendlich.* She knows that this is the beginning of my plunging into describing my dream that deals with the cardinality of continuous relations. "You must be dressed in white for this symbolic language if you want me to interpret," she says. She always goes with quantifiers, while I go with functions. I oblige. My silk is as dynamic as her logic. White *tefillin* bind my arms and my hands, while my mouth spouts distances between two points that cannot be formulated in Euclidean geometry.

After the ritual proof ceremony, I translate her meta-language into a natural language that describes my event. The story flows as a quick Heraclitean river. I lose my breath and my eyes petrify. "He came to me in my dream with his face disfigured. I laid my hands on it and he cried with joy. – "And?" she asked? "Nothing." – "And" has already occurred as a homophonic connection," I say. I pour cold water unto my head. My white hair matches my diamonds. Disjunctively, mother goes back to where she came from. He, whose face I still hold into my hands, summons the mountain for me. They both kneel. One on his knees, the other on its peaks.

COLD CASE

For Manna

It's been 12 years since my mother died. She always had a fancy for dying in such time so that she might be buried on Easter day. This actually happened. Though quite accidentally. Those believing in extra-sensory perception would say, yeah right. Those who like to fantasize would take it as an innocent coincidence. Mother fell in the second category. Though she also believed things. Like, she could never understand why every time she went to visit a friend in a nut house, the whole goddamned place would go quiet. Once she was almost offered a job there. "Imagine," the head psychiatrist said, "all the crazies gone silent without the help of pills."

But mother was anti-psychiatry. She would have liked Foucault, had she read him. Which she never did. She was more into counting. Today we do this. Tomorrow we do that. Today we remember this. Tomorrow we forget that. Mother was making history, even though she was also against history. Mother never looked behind, because she didn't want to lose life. "History, what a silly idea," she would say. "Haven't people ever heard of space?" All talk about time depressed her. That's why, to make sure that I wouldn't waste mine the day she was gone, she bought a shroud and the other arsenal that goes into a coffin time before it was needed. Like, 20 years before. The shroud was dusty and smelled of chocolate. On the catafalque, when I leaned over to kiss her cold lips, her body smelled of monoi oil. "If we can't escape death, at least we can eat it." I hear mother laughing from beyond the grave. She liked aphorisms, and so do I.

STEP AND STONE

For Sébastien

Steps. I know the sound of these steps. Keys rattling. I know the sound of these keys. Accelerated breath. I know the sound of this breath. Hesitating thoughts. I know the frequency of these thoughts. Passing. The voice passes through wires. The whistle, before the open door, ajar, transforms into a call. Telephone numbers are turned into expectation. I don't whistle. In the supermarket the mother tells her child: "don't stare at her!" The child is stubborn: "But I like her." I lean forward – while my keys rattle, while my boots make a military sound, while my breath accelerates – and whisper: "I like you too." Our eyes smile. The piper at the gate of silence needs no calls.

RETREAT

For Ursula Renz

Between the Arctic and Austria we step on stones made out of chocolate truffles. "How did you know, I ask?" and the wise woman says: "I just did." You know, she then says, "absolute nothingness is not an abstract." "I know," I say, "abstracts have forms, absolute nothingness doesn't." She nods and takes a deep breath. Mountain air is between us. We climb high and agree that closure is not in our vocabulary. I see Spinoza as the Hunchback of Notre Dame. She can also see that. Three weeks in the mountains carrying Spinoza on your back will do that to you – make you see things.

Moses Cordovero is shaking his head. "Crazy women," he thinks. And I go: "hey, you've got exactly 3 minutes to state your case." "Form is stripped away by the power of *ayin*," he says, and I ask: "where did you get that from?" But he keeps silent. "Can Kierkegaard have a word?" the other woman asks, and then says: "Don't go cosmic. Kierkegaard thinks it's a bad idea." But Kierkegaard didn't read any Freud or Lacan, so I'm not afraid. I lose my patience, and say: "all I ever want from you, men, is to answer this question: "what does it mean to say: 'I'm here,' in the light of nothingness, no point, and no form?" Isaac the Blind has an insight: "The inner, subtle essences can be contemplated only by sucking… not by knowing." We are childless women. The wise woman eradicates the materiality of time: "even if seven years pass, seven mountains are climbed, and seven oceans crossed, you come to me and say, 'I'm here,' and it will be enough." We divulge no secrets, for we are thieves in hiding.

... FOR THE MATHEMATICIAN

SET THEORY IN THREE ACTS

For Georg Cantor

ACT I

XIX

"If you so wish to construe this, I'll say this
only: the Jew is not beholden
to forgiveness, of pity. You will have to
go forward block by block, for pity's sake
irresolute as granite. Now move
to the next section."

(Geoffrey Hill, *The Triumph of Love*)

XXXV

"Even now, I tell myself, there is a language
to which I might speak and which
would rightly hear me;
responding with eloquence; in its turn,
negotiating sense without insult
given or injury taken.

Familiar to those who already know it
elsewhere as justice,
it is met also in the form of silence."

(Geoffrey Hill, *The Triumph of Love*)

ACT II

"In the Faust legend, Faust is able, with Mephistopheles' help, to take nocturnal voyages, flying through the air to other times and places and summoning scenes and personages from them to his study. He is permitted to gaze on them – to have them as sights – but other interaction is impossible, including, explicitly, speech. In the face of knowledge, Faust is silenced.

Sheherazade's position is the reverse of this. "Be silent then, for danger is in words." (V.i.27), says Marlowe's Faust to some companions before whom he is exhibiting Helen of Troy. But for Sheherazade danger lies in silence, death hovers at the edge of dawn on the horizon of light when all stories come to an end, inscribing her as well. Where Faust sells his soul for knowledge, Sheherazade saves her life by offering it."

(Lyn Hejinian, "La Faustienne", *The Language of Inquiry*)

"Authority over being is thus dispersed, not *because* of the boundlessness, but *in* the boundlessness. We don't

– as writers or as persons – go beyond "all limitations" and "all boundaries" – we enter and inhabit them. Faced with the notorious gap in meaning, we may ask, "What should we do?" But we already know what to do. And this knowing what to do is neither derived from, nor does it produce guidelines – either prescriptive, proscriptive, or even descriptive. It is, rather, intrinsic to living in context."

(Lyn Hejinian, "Reason", *The Language of Inquiry*)

ACT III

"A little knowledge is dangerous. So is a lot."

(TV-series: *Eureka*, 2006)

"So, one has to make up one's mind and have both, a little knowledge and a lot. Both this and that."

(Camelia Elias, on top of a mountain in Norway, 2008)

"But who says that either one of us has a winning strategy? The law of the excluded middle says so."

(Jaakko Hintikka, *The Game of Language,* 1983)

"Really?"

(Anonymous, c/o Curia)

EPISTEMOLOGY

For Robert Gibbons

Today I want to celebrate. Because I promised. I promised Robert a heap of words to go with his 62 years. But what words? While vacuum-cleaning the apartment, I'm thinking of entanglement. Robert likes entanglement. It's lucky that my Miele machine won't go beyond time. Robert likes time in all shapes and sizes. I'm efficient. I pick up Robert's latest book, and read the poem "The Aesthetics of the Fragment." Miele makes a noise in the background. Robert likes fragments. He also knows that I like fragments. At this point I'm trying to resist the temptation to write about myself. I'm writing a new book of poetry. The title is *In Cite.* In the new book I cite. Robert says: "I thought about the thesis, the aesthetics of the fragment. It has a lot to do with our innate refusal to see any object in some way other than inherently whole, at the same time cultivating a fondness for that which is missing, that which is consubstantial to the ruin."

In hindsight, we don't get to choose whom we cite. They choose us. Should I throw in some Lacan? – "Desire is always inscribed in and mediated by language." But Robert likes Kristeva: "significance is inherent in the human body." I have three books on my table: *Beyond Time, Epistemology: 5 Questions,* and *Becoming beside Ourselves.* They all have math in them. Which should I cite more from? I count: eeny, meeny, miny, moe. I stop after the 62nd attempt. I need to know nothing. I just desire desire. The displaced "it." Today we'll call "it" champagne. To you.

LOOP

For Anthony Johnson

In an M.C. Escher drawing, going back to square one means advancing. I'm in the scale pose, hands firmly grounded in the silken rug; torso elevated from the ground; head lost somewhere in the middle. I hear myself teaching: "if it's not good enough what you do, try again." Not many people know what M.C. stands for. Maurits Cornelis said: "so let us then try to climb the mountain, not by stepping on what is below us, but to pull us up at what is above us, for my part at the stars; amen." Maurits Cornelis's idea is seconded by that of Nick Drake, who in his collection of songs *Time of No Reply* sings these lines: "Why leave me hanging on a star / When you deem me so high / When you deem me so high / When you deem me so high." The sound comes down the spiral of no reply in threes, coming out the other side as one eloquent set: "When you hear me so clear." This is good enough for a first *échantillon* of scaling touches. Maurits Cornelis goes: "Eureka," but in the loop, the cry becomes an ecstatic "Halleluiah!"

PHYSICAL PAIN

For Horace Engdahl

You laugh the laugh of a hysterical Medusa: "I don't," you say. But I know that you do. "I can't," you say. But I know that you can. "I won't," you say. But I know that you will. This is how you formulate the meaning of life: by making suffering sovereign. Denial. Your body aches when you say: "I'm breathing." So I know that you don't. The touch that won't materialize shoots through your fantasy. It is so tender and good. My body repeats the words, "it is so tender and good." It feels the same pain. Your body feels the same "same pain" but your mouth won't say it. How to break it? I try to listen to arguments: "the life that is good must stay unchanged because it is good." My mouth repeats the words: "it is good."

In math we say that symmetry is an immunity to transformation. In literature we mess it up. There's proof. Right now, *lo and behold,* after my friend Horace has just finished bashing the Americans implicitly and explicitly by speaking in 7 tongues, and giving the Frenchy the prize, how noble of the physicists to accept the honor of receiving the laurels for their idea of breaking symmetry! The physicists explain: "at very high energy levels, electromagnetic forces, and the two atomic forces are all really the same thing. There's a deep symmetry between them. But as the energy level of the environment goes down, eventually they split, and become distinguishable. The symmetry breaks, and we get different forces."

What forces drive us? And are they high or low? The image remembers the touch, however incomplete, asymmetrical, devoid of uniform space, white, and clean, and pure. Horace would say, "bring in the psychoanalysts! Quickly. We need to apply the pleasure principle to pain." Horace says this in the language of the fragment. He was taught by Cioran, first. And then by me.

Oh, spontaneous symmetry breaking! Stop desire in transit. And let us touch it. Touch it.

LOGORHYTHMIC

For Horia Cornean

I want to say to you: "all theorems are trivial, even when they seem colossal." You will quote in turn that witty fellow of Guy Davenport: "every force evolves a form." What else is there to do, then, other than drink to that? And stuff ourselves with goat meat in ginger and turmeric. Lick our fingers afterwards, get our noses sprayed by Pol Roger, and then turn to fresh raspberries. I then see color in the black hole, and you can also swear that you see a light. Right then and there. We're ready for a cult. Our empire of the senses. A black hole has no information, so if we want to get something out of it, we had better start believing. We then go over to Taittinger and then and hence start philosophizing on identity and relationships. Then I want to say to you: "linking identity is the sum of divergence and entropy," but then I know that you will quote me: "cut the crap." So then I say instead: "Kafka was a vegetarian. And then he thought success is the biggest disappointment." My reflection in the mirror is searching for the power function of this inverted logarithm. Who wants who to come? Oh, I so do. I do. Then you will. You will.

HOLOMORPHIC

For Christoph Marthaler

The National Library. Winter time. One o'clock p.m. There is a lightning in the silence. I'm hiding behind a sheet of paper. Made in Germany some time around 1200. Matthew the Evangelist is depicted at his desk, scroll in hand, brush between the fingers. Johannes is taking a break. Hand on forehead. Thinking. Christoph and I are making conformal maps which we want to apply unto predictions. Infinity as a set in relation to exegetic hermeneutics as a set is either attractive, repellant, or indifferent. But as neither Christoph, nor I know anything about math, we have our own ways of studying sequences converging to the boundary along bubble trees. Complex analysis. While we declare that when infinity ceases to be attracting, the set gets weird, we watch the film *Harold and Maude.* On our iphones. Behind the manuscripts. He, embodying Matthew. Eyes fixing on the pristine scroll and Maude's breasts. I, embodying Johannes. Ears recalling Schubert's striking key. Getting vibrations from Harold's gut. *Das ist schön.* We wander. *Wir singen.* "I like you Harold." "I like you Maude."

ALEPH 1 TO X

For Sergio

Coming down the slope in a pink sleigh along the tall towers of San Gimignano, I feel like a thing between a ghost buster and a tomb raider. I wet my index finger to feel the direction of the wind. On this side of the road it's cold. On the other, it's hot. I let myself slide off the sledge. My forehead hits the snow. A thought spears through my heart: I'm nobody's problem. I get up and leave. And leave. And leave. In Italy I plug my finger into Cantor's navel, and feel his vibrations. His gaze lacks pagination. Death knocks. I answer: "What do you want with me?" He says: "To leave it there where you want us to leave it." The sleigh takes a turn for both ends. In the continuum, ambivalence is an anti-logic dance. I call it Aleph X.

MARCH MINDS

For H.D.

At tea with the Mad Hatter, I'm showing him my new painting, *Infinity-A-1*. "Alice, my dear, you can't count worth shit," he tells me. "That's true," I concur, and then say, "but I can interpret. Infinity is what it is. Boundless." The Mad Hatter is thinking about it. He enters in character and says, "yes." "So, you understand, then?" I ask. "Yes." My faith is strong but I need more proof. So I ask him again. "What do you understand?" "That infinity is the greater love," he says. "Good answer," I say, but then I insist. "If I told you, 'If I stood on my head for you,' what then?" "I would still love you," he says. "Good answer," I say again. "If I come or if I go, what then?" "I would still love you," he says. "If I did nothing and everything at once, what then?" "I would still love you," he says. The March Hare intervenes: "you 2 are incurable. There is 1 too many ifs in this string of topsy turvys, lovy doveys, and still bills. You both need a seminar in number theory that goes all the way. I'll teach it, if you want it, and if you don't, I won't." We switch places on the table. 6 riddles fall on the plates. 3 for us and 3 for them. They all sound the same: "What do infinity and form have in common?"

The Mad Hatter: "that we want them only thus."

The March Hare: "that they are uncountable."

The Knave of Hearts: "that they are both mature."

The Queen of Hearts: "that they both murder time."

The October Einstein: "that they are both relatively relative."

Alice in Wonderland: "that we remember *doing* neither."

IFF

For Reb Derrida

The Foot Fetishists pay me compliments, just as I'm being swept away by the Fastitocalon. "I see you not, because you won't let me," I yell in high F. Xes come out of his mouth. "Is your love as white as a foaming sea?" I ask. The floater on ocean streams gives me the rainbow look, but I see him not. "Is your desire a statutory epiphany?" I cry for an answer. I'm ready to catch its vanishing point in the infinite. I hear Lyotard dictating: "there is a language without intention that requires not religion but faith." I dip my pen into the deep ink ocean, and want to write "effigy" about edifying discourses. I misspell the first letter, as "I" writes itself in the flow. The Fastitocalon allows me to break him at "iff," when I suddenly see him in the context of his ancient history. I glimpse the wisdom of the Aspidochelone. I fall in love with water letters thus and only thus.

A(C)COUNT

For Charles

With the books it's always the same. You read, you read, you read. History repeats itself. All the time. Once there were angels as many as flies, Simic tells us. Then there were the young ones who died with passion in their blood, Blaga tells us. And I, I. I am someone's secret. I live and fly. I vacillate between the boots and the books, the cantors and the kisses. I'm forty-two, how can I still do high performance alpinism? I paint instead. People want the works. But how can I sell my Nureyev? I put on my Ralph Lauren organza and sing a Bach cantata. From the shelf that faces me, the history of madness winks. Gödel didn't think Leibniz wrote his works. Just like his precursor, who didn't think that Shakespeare wrote his. Whose works do I write? Who do I call a liar? Inside me, you're playing all of Schubert's string quartets. The cello vibrates in my head, and I can't count anymore.

IN ABSENTIA

For Vincent F. Hendricks

Incantare

I'm waiting for the logician to plug himself into some fake deconstruction on my TV. Instead we get the God talk, a second time around: "perhaps we are not meant to know certain things." Oh, really? I left my professorship in the Arctic behind for a pink meteorite hitting Grand Canyon. What explosion of yellow light! Not even the *aurora borealis* can compete – I try to convince myself. If this is a game we play, who is teaching who about the law of absence?

Convocare

Epistemology of citation: there's nothing new under the sun. "Would a book of knowledge be a sacred book?" asks Jabès, only to answer to himself, "No, because knowledge is human." The pink meteorite hit a surface creating a splashing sign. V spreads its long legs. Everything is contaminated. Says Frère Jacques: "Of course – as is always the case as soon as there is a law, *the* law – all deceptions, transgressions, and subversions are possible."

Excitare

In the church of deconstruction every word that afflicts is made to symbolize something, look like something else – that something else which is always already something else. Women as the high priests demand explanations from men. But men confuse them with Brunhilde, The Valkyrie. But this is good enough. Close enough. Nicholas Royle takes the stand: *"Excitation*: This term, in so far as it could be described as such (it would be no more a term than "the unnameable," or "deconstruction"), is pronounced so as to conceal as best as it can the heterophonic pun it nevertheless harbours, like a foreign body. Excitation, that is to say, cannot be read without a logic of ex-citation, of that which dispossesses, ex-propriates, or para-cites every citation. Excitation would have to do, among other things, with an absence of quotation marks. Be alert to these invisible quotation marks, even within a word: excitation."

The V takes her sword and swings it over the black head. Siegfried, or Sigmund, asks: "What do you want from me?" – To deconstruct "nothing."

MAGNETIC FIELDS

For Bent Sørensen

The mountains that I want to climb, and the tightrope that I want to walk, and the silence that I want to listen to – I've done it all. I go preaching in the valley: "the very condition of existence is nothingness. No-thing-ness." "Whatever," the crowd says. But this is not the same crowd as the one in Monty Python's *Life of Brian* shouting: "we are all individuals, oh, master, give us a sign, we ARE all individuals, just as you say." And Brian goes: "really?" And I go, "oy!" This is the global crowd charging me with Maxwell's equations. I have no unconditional love. I have no sons to give it to me. In reverence or hatred. And Maxwell goes, "It doesn't matter." The internet is here, the lovers are here, *Die Zauberflöte* is here, Wagner is here. Some Vivaldi, some Schubert, a shit load of Bach, and then more Bach, and yes, always and of course above all Bach – we are all individuals – yes, we never search for ourselves on google, and we never stumble on lines that insist on popping up in connection with our names, even though there's no connection. The daughters of Israel shout at me in the link: "point of no return: and you shall tell your children about Egypt." I go counting, "what are the odds?" – but probability theory has never heard of the fullness of being. And my being has been zapped. And Mozart goes, "but that's a very good thing, to be *zauber'ed, meine liebe.*" And the lover goes, "whatever it is that you want, it's never gonna happen," but what does he know, the schmuck. And then Keats goes: "I must confess, – and cut my throat, today? Tomorrow? Ho, some wine!" and Die Walküre goes: "Ho-jo-to-ho!" "and evenings steep'ed in honeyed indolence…"

Such are the times when thoughts go electrical, and I can't find my mineral water.

TOPOLOGY

For Jean-Luc Marion

Gertrude Stein is pulling my leg: "Remember narrative is continuous." And then there's Wagner, and Cantor, and Bach, and all the others. I was thinking that the only thing that beats 'and yet' must be 'both, and.' And then thus there are the others, specialists in quantum grammar. What do we do with 'and then?' – Then suddenly? Transform the status of 'nothing' into 'all?' 'All are welcome.' To do what? Transform topology into a vocabulary of thinking? Thinking about it. A direct address is a ready-made costume. "You, I'm addressing – and my witnesses are 'all' here" – Or not. The gaze can also go blank, terrified by the potential No. Not yet. So 'Nothing' would come for nothing. And yet. All that writing can vibrate for! Sense it all written on the body! Gertrude hands me a cookie made by her lover, and orders me to shut up. In transfinite arithmetic, both nothing and everything have a higher status than otherwise. The set of signification comprises the oath: Here I Am. We keep counting. Alice keeps the score. And then hands touch and the kiss is hot. We love the logic of insufficient reason.

BED OF ROSES

For Mark Daniel Cohen

I lie on my bed and am making lists of cultures I prefer. The smell culture is at the top. The touch and the taste culture compete with the visual. The culture of the sixth sense is what it is: unfathomable. Through Bach, I'm synchronizing my zero energy with that of my friend, the Cohen of New York. His body is shattered to pieces. Fragments of leg scattered in the streets of New York are gathered at the hospital, also in New York. "Something dark," he tells me. "Write something dark for me," he insists, but I can't. I think of the dark chocolate he received from his kid. A smart kid who was instructed well into the art of distinction. I'm not surprised. The Cohen is a poet, and as such he believes everything that Blake said: "Less than All cannot satisfy Man." I'm thinking of bringing Romanian pastrami and chopped liver from the deli, and the fire, storm, and salt sea in the mighty cucumber in dill. The high note of the huge tone of rose absolute in my perfume, and one which only the trained ones can spot, interferes with the indole of the almost *nature morte* of the yellow leg. What does he love and long for, this writer himself, who also believes everything that Baudelaire said about the things that have "the expansion of infinite things"? Love and longing smell of vastness. My *Rive Gauche* and the stolen *Calandre* in it orchestrate a Merovingian dance. The long-haired king accepts the gift from the Snow Queen: grace as excess. The body turns olive again. And so does the mouth after finishing with counting what the sum of nine ones times nine ones is. [111111111 X 111111111] Petals ascend and descend on the bed of elevens, heralding the Sun High-One.

MAN ON WIRE

For Philippe Petit

"My life is boring," you shout. "Boooooring!" "Sure it is," I say. "Judging by the way your arms stretch over your empty desk, head banging against it, your boredom measures exactly 220 cm. That's bad. What do you want?" "I want her, the woman on wire," you say, sobbing. "Everyday she balances on the rope that's rigged between her two balconies through her goddamn living room that it drives me crazy to know just how she does it. She always acts on her gut feeling, but only with view to making monstrously rational analyses of everything. Goddamn everything."

Are you saying balconies? Like in that Romeo&Juliet thing of a tragi-comic-romantic play, written by that queer guy? Well, go ask him, then. He'll tell you: these days, it ain't about climbing ropes up the balconies or hair strands. It's all about descending. From a balloon. A red balloon. It's in the swing. Vroom, in through the glass door, landing straight onto her goddamn wire, leaving the silk behind, gliding straight between her legs, leaving her astonished.

It's all about physics, man, and numbers! The whole of 220. Two plus two is four, and if you add the zero on top, now there is a number, glissando, and gaussian, the whole four-point formula for functions, the law of magnetism kissed on its legs."

"Oh, you're here," she'll say. "Good, let's fill this desk with a lot of clutter, and chatter, and chiming glasses of wine. We'll have Gauss wrap the balloon and tie the rope." Today boredom vanishes as we smell the gunpowder on our hands.

42

For Richard Ellis

Between numbers and aging we talk about reduced circumstances. "I'm dangerous right now," he says. "Oh really?," I reply. "And stop calling me Richard," he says. "Only mother does that." "Richard," I say, "I love being men's mother." "Nooooo," he says. "Yeeeees," I say. "Everybody loves their mother, and I want to be loved. Forever and ever." "You know what your problem is?" he asks. "Give me the word," I excitedly say. "Energy." "Nooooo" I say. "Really?" pretending that this is the first time I'm hearing about it. "And why is that a problem?" I say. "Because it's too precisely calibrated," he says. "Yes," I say. "42, that's the word". And then it hits me. "Fuck me, I'll be 42 in 7 months, and some days, and some hours, and some minutes – I'm not good at counting, and arithmetics only gives me a headache." "Fuck indeed," he says. "Drink your Guinness, then. Empty it. The glass." And I'm thinking: In *The Book of Kells,* it is written: The polar bear with pink wings will go for blood meridian.

"At the pub with the bloody feminists, you have to argue about literature. And your arguments have to be good. Really good." "Richard," I say, "I'm going to the bathroom before you piss me off." "Yes, yes, yes," he says. Molly said that too. Yes, I'm in the middle of being fucked by 42. So it goes with men and their mothers. Clever men and their mothers.

THE SOCIALITE

For E.L.H

Roskilde University

—So, you're a PhD student?
—I was one 10 years ago.
—Me too.
—Any children?
—No.
—Then you'd better hurry.
—I can't have any.
—You can adopt.
—They'd have to be special.
—I was 8 when my father died, some 55 years ago.
—I was also 8 when mine died, some 35 years ago.
—And your mother? A feminist?
—No, a Marxist.
—Marxism is artificial.
—But useful.
—I've seen my mother doing things that were not artificial.

—You mean, like hammering?
—Yes. What do you hammer on?
—Poetry.
—Why?
—I'm interested in death.
—But you're not old.
—Didn't you just tell me to hurry?
—... Wait until you're old.
—Old age has nothing good in it.
—Sure it has.
—Like what?
—Well, er, wisdom, I guess.
—Isn't wisdom a myth?
—No.
—Then, you have it?
—I suppose.
—How do you pass it on?
—Well, through my writing and teaching.
—About physics?
—Exactly.
—What else?
—Well, I don't know. You'd better ask my son.
—But I'm not asking your son. I'm asking you. What else?

—I need some air. Will you excuse me?
—Sure. Are you all right?
—No. Er, yes. I think so.
—You think so?
—I think so.

Tromsø University

—So, you're a writer.
—Not really.
—But you write.
—I analyze.
—Like that?
—Like what?
—Like Beckett.
—I like Beckett.
—You look great.
—Thanks.
—I mean, for a Beckett scholar.
—I'm not a Beckett scholar.
—You're not?
—No.
—You're really smart.
—Thanks.

—I can recite a poem for you.
—You can?
—Yes.
—About what?
—Death.
—What's it called?
—*Death, Death.*
—Go ahead.
—*Døden, døden...*
—Nice.
—Arhhhh, you know, I could... you're... I would...
—I know.
—You'd also?
—Yes.
—You can have anything. I'll give you everything. My whole life is on this phone. You can have it. Take it. Take me. Steal all my texts from it. My publishers...
—If I didn't already, have everything.
—Then you would?
—I would, for all the 15 years between us.
—Live and die.
—Your poems are so young...—
—Love and die.
—...and beautiful.
—Love and love me.

—You'll have a good death.
—You think so?
—Yes.

Dublin University

—So, you're going for professor now?
—Yes.
—Your hair turned white.
—Yes.
—But, your body.
—Yes. I look better now than at 16.
—You bet. What's the philosophy?
—In your old age, the only good thing going for you is your light weight. Be ethereal.
—Like Beckett?
—Yes.
—His stomach curved inwards.
—So it did.
—What about Gertrude?
—She didn't believe in weight.
—She must have believed in something.
—Gertrude said: "I rarely believe anything, because at the time of believing I am not really there to believe."

—Do you believe?
—In what?
—In love.
—What kind?
—The total kind. The all the way kind. The interminable kind.
—I like infinity. My own.
—My girlfriend... you're a psychoanalyst, right?
—Sometimes.
—My girlfriend, she wants commitment.
—Sure she does. Don't they all?
—Yes, so you understand?
—Sure I do.
—Then, why doesn't she?
—Because she's not so smart.
—She is.
—Then what are you afraid of?
—Children.
—Do you want them?
—Well, yes.
—Then go for it.
—You think so?
—Sure I do.
—Why?

—Do you believe in life or guarantee?
—Life.
—Then, as I said, go for it.

Helsinki University

—So, you're still doing mathematics?
—No. Never have.
—Sure you have, at all our gatherings.
—I'm more of a priest now.
—You are? What doctrine?
—The loving kind. Love thy neighbor kind.
—Whoa, Norway messed you up again?
—No.
—You're cool.
—No, really, if anything, it's arithmetics.
—Whoa, such passion.
—You think?
—Yeah, a priest with a cool head and passion for counting. Churches need that. And that body of yours!
—Yes, they allow whores in the temple now.
—I've heard.
—Isn't that neat?
—Absolutely.

—"Shall we go all wild boys,
Waiting for the end?"
—Just a smack at Auden.
—With a smack of leaf and eagle, girl.
—Professor, to you. I qualified in the Arctic.
—"Waiting for the end, boys, waiting for the end.
What is there to be or do?
What's become of me or you?
Are we kind or are we true?
Sitting two and two, boys, waiting for the end."
—What end?

... FOR THE PROPHET

IMPOTENCE

For Jessye Norman

Every Sunday I'm impotent. Like God. But I don't like to say that I'm resting my old bones when my flesh is open and sensitive, and feels the pain of what a good fantasy can provide. I can't tell you what to do. But I can tell you to stop listening to bad advice. God is also resting. He doesn't feel like being authentic, and genuine, and sincere on Sundays. Find a church and get yourself blown away by the organ. At least you'll feel something. I can't invent a new narrative. Not on Sundays. But I can say that the ones we usually serve each other are usually equally nonsensical. I can't tell you how we know what we know. But I can tell you that if something ends, it's not love that ends, but knowledge. I can't tell you what to read. Not on Sundays. But I can tell you that we keep busy with deliberating between questions: "to be or not to be, to have or not to have?" You say this and I say that. "This" is superior to "that." It's closer to thought. But equally not useful. "That" is something else. Its use value is not worth the thought, if what wraps around "that" is not "this." Gifts are important on Sundays. On Sunday you show me your gift, but I can't tell you what I think of it. On Sundays I'm silent. And demand the same. I can't listen to you. But I can tell you that I can listen to myself. On Sundays I can only love myself, however inauthentically, irreverentially, irremediably. Tomorrow it's Monday. I'll go to the opera. The drama of "naught" is never over until the fat lady sings.

BURNING

For Sadiya Hassan Jimale

I walk the streets of Nazareth. Not in Israel, but Ethiopia. It's the smell walk. Every house burns. It burns frankincense. The fumes surround my white face and make it yellow. The men of Nazareth walk in *hosgunti* and are good at addressing you literally. "You," they say all the time. All narratives are told here in the second person. Now I'm convinced that George Perec was here too. "You," the woman also says, "lift your garment, smell your own body first, and then, step into the smoke."

Autumn is the color of amber, *lacrima heliandum* is the color of my naked body, but the white incense is the best. "We do what we can," the Somali woman tells me. "Smell is distinctive in itself, but here, away from home, we make no distinctions." *"Inshallah,"* I say, and the wise woman replies in Italian, *"In bocca al lupo"*. "You smell, now" she says, but the levonah, the white incense, makes me think of *Ketav Levonah,* the White Torah. Shmuel ben Aharon-Wahli tells us that the white text is the literal text of the Torah. "The White Text is a reading of the scrolls according to the perfect image of which it writes – that being the image of Mashiyach, the complete measurement of

Man." I burn with the desire to smell, so I stop listening to his going over the Black Text. The text of sin. The black woman instructs me now, and I take her teachings to my heart. I start speaking in Latin, though. My own burning bush addresses nature with beatific boldness: *"Tu, Boswellia Sacra, a posse ad esse"*. My humble self says, *"Mahadsanid."*

THE LOVER'S DISCOURSE

For Roland Barthes

I

You know how many times we begin it? – Many.

You know how many times we end it? – Many.

You know how many times we crash and burn? – As many times as it's necessary.

Tell me, do I not know how to please you? – Today, no.

Tell me, do I not know how to make you laugh? – Today, yes.

Tell me, do I not know how to make you cry? – Today, no.

How do I live tomorrow? – Tomorrow is today.

How do I breathe today? – Today is tomorrow.

How do I love forever? – Forever is now.

To know how to give

To know how to take

To know how to know

You

II

The Rabbi Elya tells the prophet El to stop imitating Jabès in poor fashion. Done. Quoting is better. El cites from THE POWER OF KEYS: "the ditch will never be a well, O blessing of the void. The heart loves and is loved only in the body, the kindness of eyes. Truth, enemy of form, repudiates the heart."

The Rabbi Elya asks the prophet El: what did you want to touch? – The naked body.

The Rabbi Elya asks the prophet El: what have you touched? – The naked soul.

The Rabbi Elya asks the prophet El: what will you touch? – The naked image.

The prophet El issues a new prophetic vision in the form of a conclusion. All as a quotation, in inverted commas; the title, as is, and the text in jabèesquian parenthesis: "THE END AND THE MEANS (To desire something passionately means suppressing the heat of any other desire, means fusing all your desires into one, possessing nothing in order to claim everything at once. The most deprived have the maddest desires. Emptiness aspires to be filled. Wanting to be the poorest for love in order to be one day – who knows? – the most fortunate…)"

III

You follow me. I cite: *"Anoki"*. Me. *"Ana Nafshi Ketivat Yahavit."*

I take you from "me" to "I state my soul in writing."

I do.

You sign yourself over to reading.

You do.

ENVISION

For Paul David Hojda

Something flows. Knowledge has movement. The movement of knowledge is to flow towards acknowledging that there is another kind of knowing than the Socratic one. The Greek's proposition that "I know that I know nothing" is not very useful. Socrates is not thinking about knowledge in relation. But any androcentric maneuver should consider containers, counterfactuals, and contradictions. As such. And in as much.

One desires to have one's knowledge (of nothing) be contained by another's knowledge (of something). As it were. Has Socrates ever read David's song: "I am my beloved's, his desire is for me?" Seeing as becoming.

We contain knowledge and the other. There are only passages. Such as the one I quote from *Language, Eros, Being: Kabbalistic Hermeneutics and Poetic Imagination*: "whoever desires to be seen before his master should not enter except by means of this stone." The pronoun "this" takes the feminine form (zo't). It is through the *Shekhinah*, the gateway to dwelling, that one gets to know about dwelling. "Communion can ensue only from envisioning, and envisioning only from communion."

Envision the secret of the rainbow. The telephone rings. My nephew plays a Satie piece on the piano for me, and then whispers: "You know, I adore you." I know.

BLESSING

For Ioana

I summon myself on the wizard's threshold. I bring blessings: blessed be the virgin, blessed be the child, blessed be the man who loves so much that he can't tell the difference anymore, blessed be the woman who loves so much that she can't tell the difference anymore. And yet. Meanwhile, I sound like a Catholic. Blessed be the cat. Blessed be the mat. I sound like a structuralist. Saussure went bonkers from reading signs. It is not the sign that keeps us sane, but feeling. Painted with cosmic vibration. The color is yellow and white, white and yellow. The white makes room for red. "There is a Text in women," Alexander Niccholes writes in 1615. *Paradise Regained* was also written in 1600s. "I see thou know'st what is of use to know." Hold on to that. Hold on to the text. Hold on to the books. A whole library of touches. Real touches. Sublime touches. Painful touches. Readable touches. In *The Book of Touches* it is written: I shall not let you dangle in the air, but bless you. I shall not let you suffer alone, but bless you. I shall not let you love in silence, but bless you.

TRAINS

For Jim Canary

Botticelli did it. Tintoretto did it. Poussin did it. Trainspotting. Red silk all over the place. I see you see me. Thy hand in mine. Thine eyes dipped in color. Scrolling. Rolling. "Whither goest thou, America, in thy shiny car in the night?" Botticelli had it. Tintoretto had it. Poussin had it. I snatch your red book. You want it back. The dictionary reminds us: *memento mori,* while we lament: so what, then what? Time bound. Ditch the clock. Let color rule. You have numbers on your chest. I inhale, you exhale. Your hand be-gloved. I beg. "The world would never find peace until men fell at their women's feet and asked for forgiveness." Inverse order. Your gaze in mine, unbound. The train makes a sound. Botticelli knew it. Tintoretto knew it. Poussin knew it.

STAR WARS: A PURPLE TRILOGY

For the Jedi Knights

Episode I - Illuminations

You said yes to everything even before I opened my mouth. Then, when I did open my mouth, fragments came out if it. Now I want to yell at myself: "how are you going to make the fragment compatible with everything?" Someone bring in the mathematicians. Quickly! Meanwhile, I'm looking for a hammer that's bigger than Nietzsche's. No, wait, make it a lightsaber. Someone let me smash the fragment in the name of everything. The fragment raised to the power of maximum. Illuminated. When the time is right the maze will turn into a window. You will come out of the penumbra. Ready for an outbound flight.

Episode II - Dances

Jedi Ezra Pound is patrolling my site in his Star Cruiser. Jedi Junior Charles Olson is learning the craft of incantation.

The *Maximus Poems* are born. By hand. I cite with an ax in my eye:

> One loves only form
> and form only comes
> into existence when
> the thing is born
> born of yourself, born
> of hay and cotton struts,
> of street-picking, wharves, weeds
> you carry in, my bird
> of a bone of a fish
> of a straw, or will
> of a color, of a bell
> of yourself torn.

Master Yoda Wittgenstein sends Pound and Olson a telepathic question: "are you serious?" followed by an instruction: "Here's how we think of quantifiers around here. 'The sword Excalibur consists of parts combined in a particular way. If they are combined differently Excalibur does not exist.'" I ask the master, "ah, so you're a dancer? Do you know what Confucius said?" Wittgenstein is thinking about it.

Episode III - Erudition

I, Queen Gertrude Anscombe – you can call me Elizabeth – am X'ing intentionally.

Master Yoda Wittgenstein lying on the lawn of the excluded middle wants to know: "Are you The First Person?"

Jedi Ezra Pound sends him a telepathic thought from the starship Maximus: "She is The First Person", only, since he's been cruising in circles and got dizzy, he confuses Queen Gertrude with the Writer Gertrude, the Other Yoda Stein, Gertrude Stein, who made him kneel and acknowledge her mastery. *Fierfek!*

I, The intended First person, The intentionally Second Person, and The Third Person intentionally intended ask you three: is the following Yodantic question the right question: "When all choices seem wrong, choose restraint?"

(*Blast! By the Abyss!* The Queen, in her capacity as The Third Person is thinking that the First Person is just about to commit the moral fallacy formulated thus by the Second Person: what do you care about what the right question is, when all consequentialism is purple?)

INVOCATION

For Quintus Horatius Flaccus

Randolph: "The whole of you, the depth of you, called to me."

Christabel: "You take me out of myself and give me back — diminished — I am wet eyes — and touched hands — and lips am I too — a very present-famished-fragment of a woman."

I: "If it happens it happens, and if it doesn't it doesn't."

You: "It has to happen."

I: "And then, you say it will die forever?"

You: "Yes"

I: "Really?"

You: "…"

I: "The eyes, then, can I touch them?"

You: "Yes"

I: "Now?"

You: "Yes"

I: "Then, it happened?"

You: "Yes"

I: "Veni vidi vici."

You: "Vocatus atque non vocatus Deus aderit."

I: "..."

Cecilia Bartoli: "Quella fiamma che m'accende."

TRIBES

For Kathleen Gibbons

I'm having Stilton blue cheese marinated in port wine, with a shot of 70 percent slivovitch, 2 times distilled. Tribal knowledge. While I think that I should get paid heavy money for my invention, I go back to thinking about church. I think of churches I've been to, and on Sundays I paint them with the twelve tribes of Israel in mind. The first two in the series are awaiting the rest of the company. Asher, who plotted to sell his brother Joseph into slavery gets this blessing from his father, Jacob: "From Asher will come the richest food; he will provide the king's delights." I take another bite of cheese, and with Benjamin in sight, I imagine my spirit poured from the silver cup hidden in his sack. I'm having a hard time seeing him as a ferocious animal. But not his father, obviously, since he issued this vision for him: "a vicious wolf, devouring the prey in the morning, and dividing the spoil at night." I see Benjamin as the son of my yoga master, Kathleen, whose golden hair and a body to die for, inspires to things beyond sins. The silver cup turns into gold. I leave the company of thieves and traitors, and start seeing the best in everything. Joseph blesses me: "act as if what you want is already true." I go ask my gut feeling what that is.

DIAMOND CUT

For Dora

My lava jewelry is sunk into the blue lagoon. What stands between my ring and my now steamy golden watch is a poem. Audre Lorde in astrakhan black coat, black goggles, and black hair has diamonds in her mouth. Some sight.

 I
is the total black,
being spoken
from the earth's inside.
There are many kinds of open
how a diamond comes
into a knot of flame
how sound comes into a word, coloured
by who pays what for speaking.
Some words are open like a diamond
on glass windows.

I kiss my chess playing sister before she goes to work. I open the door for her." Then the window. On the threshold she tells me what the word is. Paul in Acts 18 had a vision: "do not remain silent." I think about that. But how to reclaim someone else's word? And I also want to claim Lorde's word: "Love is a word, another kind of open." The Bible is on the table. I open it and Proverbs 24 unfolds: "A wise man has great power; and a knowledgeable man increases strength."

I prefer the prophets to the converted patriarchs. Wisdom is a polished jewel in the open morning. It's seven, my watch tells me. Its name is Omega. But time reflected in the diamond is boundless. Lord-less. The lava bedevils me. It's coffee time.

DIVINATION

For Andra Jakstaite

I am the diviner. The wandering rabbis search for wells, but only I know how deep they are and where they are. In their order of things, they go ahead, I go behind. In my order of things, they don't even exist – lavish absence. This is a syllogism of the suspended middle. I integrate faith and reason in a way that the patriarchs don't. But they still need me to tell them how grace can remain a free gift. The word is made strange in their scrying. "Who has ever heard of a feminist diviner?," they ask. That's because I don't believe in their stolisomancy, sortilege, and scarpomancy. "What's the word for today?" they ask. And I say: "Mercury. Have you ever wondered why he's always depicted on one foot? On top of a building, if a statue? Get your cameras and shoot the one in Copenhagen." "Oh, come on," they go. "Why do we have to do this?" – Because it's spring, and because you're poets.

ENTHRAL

For Geoffrey

"Thing": id est, thinking or think'd. Think, Thank, Tank – Reservoir of what has been thinged. – Denken, Danken, – I forget the German for Tank/The, Them, This, These, Thence, Thick, Think, Thong, Thou"

Coleridge in his Notebooks didn't put a full stop after this string. So this is not hermetically closed. Thinking knows no hermeticism. Silent speech aims at a punctum. "AND YET: is not writing too much with us?" asks Hartman in *Saving the Text*. So, no full stops after the inscription on the body. The palm carries the lines of the "Thing." I drop my ring into my glass. The thought is not hermetic.

Outside my house, near the supermarket, there is a huge circle on the pavement. Every day I'm waiting for "Them" to paint the letter H inside it. The "Thing" is a helicopter. The "Thought" is militaristic: "you are ordered to come now." And "Thou" shall not ask "This" stupid question again: "Really?" "Danke" I say. For what, I don't know. I'm saving the revelation for later.

TOUCHING PERSEUS

For Ruth Gordon

Up north the stars shoot from the gut. Some claim it's Perseus's nether region that does it. I look at it, and look at it, and look at it some more. Some call this star gazing. The temperature goes down. I feel the zero on my toes. I make a wish. With my eyes closed. So it can't be gazing that does it. Make it true. I know it. With my eyes closed I focus on my breath. My breath in art. Perseus may be well endowed, but it's his navel I'm interested in. It smells like dark chocolate made with cardamom seeds. I have them on my tongue. The seeds. Their smell is the smell of our mixed blood. It comes out of my nostrils. I exhale - - - Your shirt goes up. I breathe into your navel. You're waiting for my touch. Your whole body aches with memory and desire. I touch you, and you swoon. I touch you again. Your eyes open, and you swear on the stars that I am It. Not the stoning Medusa, but the other one. The secret one. The one with the trumpet, whose blow is a Gorgoneion apotropaic gaze that turns stone into a starring touch. You saw it. You felt it. You loved it. You want it. The foursome crystal constellation.

CONTACT

For Waltraud Meier

Earth to Jupiter. The 6000 needles piercing my body as I lie on my shakti mat shake my visual memory. Is there contact? There was nothing on the sky last night, but I can see now that Orion chased someone else. Not very far. A torrent of meteorites must have hit you on your head. Your head close to mine. Your small bone structure is vibrating. Numbers align themselves on the black. I won't call. I hate telephones and dialling numbers is most quaint. I prefer other gadgets. My mind mostly. It can conjure constellations. In them my power over you is as endless as your love. No one can mess with Frigg's distaff.

POETRY'S TOUCH

For Blaise Pascal

Here comes Keats, who didn't get to live the sexual revolution. Keats was into hands; hand-writing, and hand-touch. Keats couldn't make himself say, 'how about it?' like a moron, after the sublime silence trespassed the embarrassing threshold of 'how about it, then?' Lo, the feminists had a point: if you can't find someone worth fucking, go fuck yourself. Very good point. Keats, can you hear that? I hope you're turning in your grave as I bend over it, passing some good feminism over to you. Here comes Keats, whose "Living Hand" instils in me visions of caressing balls, if that is what the man wants, however vulgar and much in vain. But poetry can make anything vibrate. Listen to this:

> This living hand, now warm and capable
> Of earnest grasping, would, if it were cold
> And in the icy silence of the tomb,
> So haunt thy days and chill thy dreaming nights
> That thou would wish thine own heart dry of blood
> So in my veins red life might stream again,
> And thou be conscience-calm'd – see, here it is –
> I hold it towards you.

Halleluiah, I feel touched! I'm writing this to myself now. No one else. Norway, here I come, to fuck myself, and your sheep, and your provincialism, and your highest peak! Norway, I swear by your orgasm that although I can see that you don't fall for all this piss that Keats is talking about, you can also see that this hand of mine will henceforth overcast and cancel all your Novembers.

> But if you'd try this: to be in my hand
> as in the wineglass the wine is wine.
> If you'd try this.
>
> *wie im Weinglas der Wein Wein ist.*

– I go to bed drunk with Rilke under my pillow. I still know what I know.

It snows, but I'm not cold anymore.

IN SIGHT

For Henrik Godsk

After staring long enough at Rembrandt's great painting *The Jewish Bride,* while also reading essays from Gabriel Josipovici's book *Touch,* I feel touched in more than one way. I imagine being both of Rembrandt's models at the same time. The man and the woman. With my hand on the torso I imagine feeling its heat and vibrations. I keep the stroke steady to feel the smoothness, the silky surface, and the flow of the body. With my hand on the other's hand, I imagine feeling its lines striving for something that is both natural and momentous.

There is a complicit doubleness in touch as it confirms its own presence. "Its presence to you, but also its presence to it," says Josipovici. As I throw myself at plagiarizing Rembrandt, I think of miraculous touches, yet the ones whose healing powers are felt only as a form of longing. I paint as Bach's *Toccata,* another form of touch, pounds into my ears. The sounds connect to the orbit of my attention, and I drop some eyes onto the canvas. I want to be tender to them, but I also feel the urge to stick them out of their fixation. But the power of the gaze beyond boundary wins. I close my eyes and feel touched by the eloquence of such (in)sight.

MIRROR

For The Three Musketeers

I'm looking into a mirror that's not mine. But what I see is not a reflection. I touch the hair and it is mine. The red lips are mine, and so is the small body. I throw myself onto the polar bear skin to feel the geometrical surface of multiplied illusions. Face down. My chest is not flat. Nor is it that of a madonna. I'm 16 again, dreaming of riding white horses and rescuing male damsels in distress. I'm plugged into something that my spinal cord identifies as "it." "You're perfect," the mirror says, from an angle that bypasses the law of the excluded middle. I believe it. The middle itself tells me that I should.

... THE FOOL

PAN PAJAMAS

For Peter Lax

Phony. This is the word that I like and dislike. In the age of information originality is not original. Take Julian Schnabel's walking around in pajamas – because his young wife designed them nicely, he claims – every time there is a vernissage he has to show up to. Of course he got the idea from Matisse who was a real pajamas lover. Although I never wear pajamas – I'm into naked bodies – I'm thinking of getting one from amazon.com. Marilyn Monroe pajamas – which makes me think about that famous picture of her reading *Ulysses*, and which nobody can understand. I'm sure that if she wore pajamas instead of hot-pants, people would stop going round in the hermeneutic circle. The unreality of some things is just mind boggling. I'm gonna go read Roger Penrose's latest *The Road to Reality* that has everything in it, from fractions to fiber bundles. If Julian, Henri, Marilyn, Roger, and myself go bundling I'm pretty sure that we'll hit a spot of knowledge. Fractions by night. Information can go fuck itself.

WELT IM BLAUEN

For Anonymous

Upon seeing Per Kirkeby's series of five paintings at Louisiana, Wald-variation, the one in the middle recalls for me a Shakespearian setting. Thinking of architecture, I turn to my husband and tell him: "there's Romeo and Juliet's Verona." While admiring what in my head are three arcades, I continue saying that I can almost hear Juliet's dress swishing on the traversing balcony. Although Kirkeby's main color is green, I see Juliet's dress as blue as the blue Tiziano used in his depiction of Ariosto. "Arcades?", my husband goes. "Forget setting. What you see is Romeo, Juliet, and Anonymous." "Woa, some revelation," I think to myself. The setting falls into the background. Sex and sensuality emerge from the image. I see myself at home. "Which of the two," I ask? "We'll have both," he says. Sometimes husbands have all the right answers. First Juliet died. Then Romeo died. Juliet did it again, shortly after her resurrection. We don't know what happened to Anonymous. This uncertainty builds on architectonic knowledge. The window of opportunity is open towards the world of potential not the world of principle. Was it this that made *Orlando Furioso?*

FORUM

For Avital Ronell

Another cantor follows me. Leonard Cohen bows and says: "I'm your man." Leonard knows a thing or two about bowing. He is convinced, as he repeats it three times, that "there ain't no cure for love." As a psychoanalyst, I am, of course, of a different opinion. But I like his dedication to all things naked that we desire to touch just for the heck of it. The heightening of emotion requires no plans, no questions *à la* "and how should I then presume?" You can't condition emotion if you want to learn something about the ineffable. Adore it only. Leonard, the seducer theologian and high priest, is not waiting for any miracles, to all his ladies' astonishment, who keep asking him: "what is all this good for?" "Nothing and everything," Leonard says, secretly wishing that this line was his invention not Camelia Elias's. But Camelia knows what made Leonard climb the Hubbard glacier that stands between Canada and Alaska. She knows the significance of the middle. She knows how to be in the miraculous middle.

As Cohen is asking 7000 Danes gathered at the Forum whether they want to know what the meaning of life is, Elias is the only one who knows the answer before hand.

The back singers sing: te dum, te dum, te dum, te dum. Leonard picks up the line and says: "too dumb." The crowd laughs, but it has no idea what it is that's laughing at. Camelia has Paul Muldoon in her pocket. In his poem, *Madoc: a Mystery,* charting the history of ideas where everybody from Heraclitus through Zeno and Thales to Simone de Beauvoir, Lacan, Derrida, Tarski, Popper, and Quine meet, Muldoon pays tribute to Cantor and Gauss, (Camelia's favorites), by joining in the choir of *illuminati* and singing louder than everybody else at the refrain "de dum," thus proleptically anticipating Leonard's: "too dumb".

Muldoon and Elias have met before, at tea with Gertrude Stein and cookies made by Gertrude's lover. Muldoon remembers how the four of them "sat in the nude round the *petit fours* and repeated Eros is Eros is Eros. If he had to do it all over again he would still be taken in by her Alice B. Toklas Nameless Cookies and those new words she had him learn: hash, hashish, *lo perfido assassin.*"

QED

For Edna St. Vincent Millay

The internet is down. The TV is down. The telephone is down. Am I dead? But I can't see myself in the ground. Not while I'm blasted by Vincent Lübbeck's organ works, after a round of three sets of listening sessions to *Die Zauberflöte* in a row. The *umlaut* over the letter "u" means that the door is open. I blow a whisper through the flute. "O" that goes through "ö" marks a traversing movement from wonder to doubt. O, to learn more, or ö, is it worth it? What can a master in ambivalence teach? To go with it, say a silent *yes* to everything and nothing, but also simultaneously leave it at that, say a silent *no* to nothing and everything? "It" and "that" are unknowns.

I call on Jabès who is the key master of cryptic texts. He can even open non-knowledge. Non-knowledge is, of course, not ignorance. It is silence. How Jabès makes sense of silence is mind boggling. 20 years I've been thinking about it – and him. And I'm not even dead yet. Jabès says: "Knowledge is extreme poverty of power." And then, "They turned their spotlights on the eroticism of the word, but it was the eroticism of silence that dazzled." "They" refers to the lovers in *The Book of Ques-*

tions, an earlier text by Jabès, which he brings in sight. I cite this text while peeping through its hole, the parenthesis that Jabès uses to **sOrround** it, so that I don't get enlightened all at **Once**. O, staying at the margins! Non-knowledge is here present and it guides my reading: *("The most erotic minute is the chalky minute of silence," Yukel had noted. "But lust is waves of sweat foaming with sperm," said Yaël once. "Unforgetable nights. You write with sperm on the beautiful moist pages of my glistening body." And right after, as if in a dream: "Lust is a mortar binding the stone.")*

I'm reading from *The Book of Margins.* How do I answer its charges? I know. I embody the missing visual technology, so I can mirror what I'm doing. I cut a hole in my bra and let the silence in my bosom burst through it. Men take a plunge and pay tribute to silence by sucking what "it" gives off itself through the hole. I analyze the situation. There is a trema over the letter "e" in Yaël. I transliterate the Romanian "I", eu, into ëü. Something has just opened. My mouth. It articulates: "It" is ëü-phoric. "That" you can bet on, echoing Edna:

> Of light anatomized! Euclid alone
> Has looked on Beauty bare.

I'M HERE

For Watt

Beckett from across three pages, which I try to read at the same time – while three candles burn, while Bach pumps the organ, while my friend updates his status on facebook emphasizing that he likes to listen to Rabbi Elias talking incessantly, but that he also likes the Rabbi to get crushed by Bach, so that some silence can occur, while I listen to my friend and get astonished again and again because he gets it, all of it, and more so, while reading lumpy poems on the silly lumpy pudding website, while the organ suddenly takes over and the toooootally fat sounds hit me in the guttest of my gut, especially the uterus as the more anatomically specific oriented would have it, while my body sinks under heavy-weight thinking, and yet also floating in the air at the idea that all we have is words, performance, and costumes to enact the sublime, man, what bullshit, but we buy it, we buy all of it, because we sense it, man, how we sense it, that it almost makes us think that there must be more between heaven and earth, but there isn't really, it's all projections and mirrors, and man, how we want the best, the very very very best, the absolute best, the highest best, even Jesus said verily verily, the best exists, because we believe it, man, can you believe that, that is just so astonishing, believing while remaining silent in the face of knowing that the other knows that one is ready already for the already, the already that has already happened, fuck man, where is Derrida when you need him to tell you that it's all very unique in that very deconstructive way, and sublime too, and verily and verily worth the while, but then he was a Romantic – Beckett says on the first page, because I can't really read three pages at the same time, it's all a bluff, Beckett says: "You're on earth. There's no cure for that."

FOLDS

For Ida

The bed-sheets are white. The big book is black. Between them the body is naked. My white silk morning robe is at the house by the sea. I project reality between fire and knowledge. In reality I wear my lush silk everywhere. Also in dreams. I want salt in my hair. The sand is white. The sky is white. The zero degree temperature makes my hands white. I stick my pink toes into the water. The wind blows into my white wrap around. The peasants also possess knowledge. They are convinced that they see a crazy cosmopolitan. They nod. They know one when they see one. In the book of Romans it is written: "whatsoever is not of faith is sin." The clash of opposites, *antitheta*, is the most effective form of verbal eloquence. I enunciate into their mute faces: "I have faith." The wind blows the silk onto my face. I make sinful analogies. Of the fluid kind. Knowledge flows between our legs. Fire burns our heads. The book to ashes. The silk syncopates a fold. I hold on to it.

DESCENT

For Rosalyn Tureck

I watch Eve Sussman's film. *The Rape of the Sabine Women.* The banquet. I'm in it – the film. Astrakhan coat in hand. I lament my existence while also lying on the bean bag. Gazing. I imagine being the artist who turns yellow 60s dresses into stone. The Sabines are fighting their fathers. Their brothers. The whole world's stupidity. It all becomes dust. Sculpted dust. I stick my hand into my pants through the silence of the lambs. The Sabines approve. From the next room I imagine Anonymous descending from my Romeo and Juliet tableau. He's here. My mind gets filled with desire. We're going to do the Hockney together. No Velazquez for us. We're too cosmic for him. The mirrors are good, but the eyes are better. My starship is landed in his.

RED REDUX

For Julie Kavanagh

The red strawberry stops between my teeth just before my fingers have a chance to push it further into my mouth. I'm watching Nureyev's dance of the knight. "O Romeo, Romeo, wherefore art thou Romeo?" Juliet's dress is kissed with reverence. The strawberry falls between my legs. My eyes are fixed on him. But in my memory I see that his bodily movements are not those in his beloved painting by Fuseli: *Satan Starting from the Touch of Ithuriel's Spear.* I'm looking for a dark touch of this illustration for Milton's *Paradise Lost* in Nureyev's Shakespearean Gothic Romanticism. But all is pink. "Pale pink ballet slippers could be yours for just 50 dollars." They are, according to Christie's auction catalogue, "considerably soiled and worn." The Montagues ladies swish their garments against those of the Capulets. Legs go left, then right. My hand goes up and down between my thighs. The strawberry resists being found. *Viola d'amore* picks up Prokofiev's dramatic tune of "da." Da-a-a-a. My mouth, still open, articulates: "what am I saying yes to?" Nureyev's legs open wider. So do Juliet's. And mine too. We're all ready for the red touch. Re-speared. Re-souled. Re-soiled. Re-sealed. Sold.

HEEL

For Hélène Cixous & Kathleen Ferrier

From where we stand – always in square one – always before the beginning – always before the end – always under the spell – always in the middle of the greatest passion – always dialectically vigilant – but deconstructive – you give me your love – always conditioned by the unconditional – by everything and nothing. We are in the subplot of *Don Quixote,* when Quixote reads about himself – in *Hamlet's* subplot, when Hamlet gazes on himself, how spectacular! – in the 602nd story of the *Arabian Nights* 1001 cycle, when the king hears about the murderous but desirous king, himself. It's all about penetration. "I can't let you be part of my life," you say, while penetrating mine, while doing it all the time by opening a door made out of flesh and bones. My clavicle feels the warmth of your hand like a penetration. My hand on your hand consolidates the magic. – *Salve! Orbis terrarum est speculum Ludi.* We are X-ing the geometry of the point, repairing the intentional fallacy that left Achilles' heel without coverage. Spot on, we penetrate the heel with our gaze, healing it, so Achilles can run faster from the time that stands still. From where we stand, we read about ourselves in the most magical of all touches.

FRENCH WINDOWS

For Gabriel Josipovici

Two doors.
Glass first. Seeing through.
Then stone. Silence.
Two people on the threshold.
Two fingers on the buzzer.
One to the left. One to the right.
Going through.
Smiles. After you, Madam!
Nodding. Silence.
A touch on the door-handle. Untouched.
A ring. Unrung. Silence.

A page. Ripped out. Passing through.
Everything passes.

The wind in the hair. You're obsessed with my hair. Silent.
Under the hair is the head. Silent.
Pure thought.
You would give anything to have me. Silent.

I chair the panel on cosmic relations.
He says: Cormac McCarthy says, "so be it."
I think Vonnegut says, "so it goes."
He says: Cormac McCarthy says, "there is hope."
I say: in the face of "so be it"?
He says: Joseph McElroy says, "there is energy."

Everything passes.

He says, "cosmic obsession doesn't."
I say, "is that of love, of writing, or doors?"
Silence.
He says, "Shakespeare knew his audience. Rabelais didn't."
He says, "Shakespeare was obsessed with love. Rabelais with writing."
I, with doors.
I would think anything to touch you. Silent.

Writing is silent. You step behind the curtain of the French window. My shadow is grey. Silent. On my sleek stockings with a black seam that ends in a doodle it is written: "Stop," on one leg. "Go," on the other.

I pass, but not from your mind.

NORWAY: THE SUM OF CONVERGENCES

For Johan Schimanski

Norway! – you make my passions stream through my nostrils while also making me think that whatever thought is, it doesn't matter.

Norway! – your mossy green sticks to my eyes and your smell hits me hard in my gut turning it into Babylon.

Norway! – I speak your tongue but my phonetic rules are transgrammatical.

Norway! – your sheep and goats acknowledge my presence which makes me grab them by their hind legs and turn them on their heads so that their bleating can score a higher pitch. The less banal is constructed without sacrifice.

Norway! – I want to go to Tromsø where all the boa-deconstructors went. Su-pli-ca-tion. They all believed in supplication. I want to believe in supplication. The boas in the temple of silence, counting on meshless methods.

Norway! – your *aurora borealis* makes me crazy. Cra-zy. I point three fingers at the absent trees and think that I'm Huldra. Invisible to all, but my own fingers. Your winds touch them, your waters love their caresses, your forests eat them getting intoxicated.

Norway! – if you were not Norway, I would be Norway, allowing tourists and lovers like myself to enter me only on the 12th of the month, each year, each century, each hour. On the 12th hour love time is camping time. The million of Dutch drivers passing through you can testify.

Norway! – I want your peaks to be hot saunas, and your lakes monoi oil on my body.

Norway! I love you, as I spit into your rivers thinking:

Panta rhei.

FLESHED-OUT

For Rainer Kaus

The pathology of big breasts is going out. "Who do you want to look like?" the head plastic surgeon asks me. I know exactly so I answer unhesitatingly. "Well, like those two gnomic gnats, Beckett and Bob Dylan." "Who," he asks again? "Beckett and Bob Dylan," I say, and refrain from offering additional information. This strategy is also part of the program, to keep it simple. I go for the slender androgynous look. My hair will also turn completely white in six months, so I'm ready to face the world in this final phase of my meaningful or meaningless existence. "Say what?" Beckett asks me, and he never makes any conversation that is not based entirely on body language and no words. I say nothing. Ten vectors of ten-second thoughts go through my mind. Number two has this in it: *O, yes, yes, of course, why not, how excellent, this is just brilliant, it can't get any better that next time, when men tell me that they respect me, they will not mean the exact opposite. And they will not look at their watches in my presence either.* Dylan intercedes on thought number five: "A poem is a naked person. Some people say that I am a poet." *Good then, we go with that,* number one thought dictates, as number one never has anything original to say.

My scurrilous intelligence is being performed on at the level of flesh. The less of it, the higher ground. "Have you been reading about Estragon and Vladimir on the verge of hanging themselves only so that they can get a major erection?" Beckett wants to know. But all I say is this: "I disappear a lot," just when my hand is being twisted by the good doctor who says: "Not bad. Not bad at all." Dylan goes, "Pressing On," and I think: *Fucking Freud is home.*

BONNE CHANCE

For Fabiana Heifetz

I have banging Eros on my head on the way to see Grand Canyon. The one over here, not the one over there. The Hockney thing. So, I walk up the path, and down into the garden, and up again, and past the grill, past the Chinese little girls who start following me saying hi all the time, once they finish rolling in the grass, and past the past. There is a direct line from Hockney's purple and straight into the bathrooms. And you never know who you can ambush there. Smoke envelops me and I hear the erudite one saying: "Cosmic constellations. There are causal relations that are above us." I look at him sideways and wonder if he has just been reading Eric Hoffer, who was also into literary orbiting: "We can be absolutely certain only about things we do not understand." "Is that cosmic enough for you?," the one still here asks.

Ah, the embrace, and the kiss, and the knowledge. "That's more than enough – I hope." I say this with strong conviction and emphasis on "hope." Smoke envelops us, and the one who got to me through Derrida, Great Jascha's relation tells me: "You're here because I summoned you." "Oh, really?," I ask and then she goes: "You know, some women think that Lacan was *un hombre muy hermoso.*" Echolalia is in the air: *"Je dis toujours la verité. C'est les mots qui manquent."* – Palavre of the handsome one. "Boof," the owl goes. *"Bufnita"* and *"polonic"* are the best Romanian words. "Are they?," Borges's translator wants to know, and she offers *"horoscopul"* as a worthy competitor. "Of course she *"ul",* wouldn't she?," I think to myself, and start enumerating the languages that she can speak. Many. "I'll come to your place and bring luck," she says. *Bon.* Meanwhile, all I can think of is the image she offers me: I, as a rich Lebanese heiress in the presence of the king of deconstruction. Some are laughing, some are squinting, and for the life of me, I have no idea what keeps Eros so long.

LIMIT

For Sophus Lie

Through the mists of Avalon, all for you, I go from doing backbends in the old cemetery to supplicating, also on my back, and also for you. Where goes the limit? The one to waiting? The one to knowledge? I take another cherry. A grotesquely big one. This is a bloody affair. My fingers get stained. But I lick them with such passion and speed. With my eyes closed, and mouth full of the red stuff, I suspend the ground between my youthful body, a gift of nature, and my white hair, a work of art. Eating shifts what tilts the dominant pendulum. All for you, but whether thus or thus? Between ontology and epistemology my gut opens itself like a gorge to give a façade to the limit. I have become a wall through which you pierced a nail. I hang my questions on it. You wail and wait.

CAVEAT

For Truls Mørk

My time to move to Norway has not come yet. But today I lent my body to Schubert. Schubert, who always wanted to be a woman. I said: "Schubert, my love, take my body and your soul to Norway. Away from gatekeepers, peer-reviewers, false-prophets, schmucks, rationalists, and literalists. There you can be the woman you want be. And no one will notice. There will be no one." Schubert said yes. To thank me, he wrote the *adagio* for me. To evacuate my death.

THE TROMSONIAN

For Roald Amundsen

Rachmaninov's third concerto has come to Troms. "The Snow Queen will be attending," the whispers go. On the stage, the Polar Explorer takes a deep bow. He squints at her majesty's white dress and yellow cape. She sends him an electrifying look that zig-zags his pupils. "You have no idea what I'm capable of," he responds telepathically. She starts laughing so hard that the entire front-row vibrates with renewed energy. It's a good thing that she has all the seats reserved for herself, so that no one else can catch her face in embarrassing astonishment. How is this possible? You can't do the fat notes with slim fingers. It's just not possible. But he's stubborn. He did after all conquer the North Pole. I'll show her. A deep breath replaces the scepticism. Disbeliefs are shattered to splinters. Bonds are sealed. Faith confirmed. Daisies are placed over the winner's eyes. The cold mouth turns red when a finger is stuck in it. The ghost-dog goes "wuf," accompanying the final smooch. The crowd empties its pockets of pink snow flakes. Polarities converge in the hoods.

FEDERMAN DIES

For Raymond Federman

Nobody ever waits. Waiting is the hardest. And you decided to die on me just like that. Well, you have been dying for some time now, just like a few people I know. Mother was dying before she actually did it, some 20 years before. The same with Beckett. By the way, say hello to both. Perhaps you can instruct mother to start reading some Beckett while there, wherever it is that you've all gone. She was a Beckettian to the bone, only she had no idea. I've also been dying since the day I was born, so we have that in common. I came into this world two months before my time. Mother was sure I was going to die. Me too. And then with all the operations, it's a miracle anyone survives. Three times I've had to spread my legs for the gynaecologist and anaesthesiologist. And then the energy thing. The ablation, they call it. Pumping up the heart to 400 beats so that they could guess where the current was, and burn its many passages. Six places they've burned it, chasing it in the dark. Which is why the current comes back, I can feel it. I'm ergodic proof of what instability means. And now I also want to get rid of my big tits. I have plastic reasons for it. I'm into the arts now. I want to seduce only myself, not others. And I fancy a splash of imitation. Beckett, whom we both love – that's right, I want to look just like him. I wonder what you'd say of that, that I may die, finally, with my chest cut open. Who's to say, indeed? We all die anyway. But meanwhile on your death, I've no idea why that obscene song sung by Serge Gainsbourg and Brigitte Bardot comes to my mind. *"Moi non plus,"* he says. *"Je t'aime,"* she says. But he insists. *"Moi non plus."* Ah, well, people come, people go. You were never sentimental about that. And yet you made me soft in my knees. Your texts still vibrate through me. The words. I'm doing a painting for you now. I use mostly the color called viridian. Can you believe such a name? You would like it, particularly because I got the inspiration from my favourite perfume, *YSL Rive Gauche.* Total viridium. So, who will read at your funeral? I'm busy writing, and feeling sorry for myself, so I'll absent myself. Goddamned it, Raymond. You could have waited for me. You make me say, *"moi non plus."* You exit, but I promise, I'll take care of the X.

STRAW

Für Anselm Kiefer

A sea of love. There must be a sea of love behind it. "It's chess" the blood relation says. "Don't touch it," the gatekeeper says. "Why not? This hair is made of straw, Margarethe's hair is made of straw." "Because Anselm won't like it." "We don't speak Danish," the chess lover says. "No, but you understand it. Now move away." "Yes, sir, Hitler sir," we say in perfect Danish and vanish in Shulamit's painting.

In the alcove where the *Ice and Blood* awaits, I hear the sister of mercy asking: "What do you see?" The alcove's resonance goes like a bullet through the surface, it ricochés on the hero's palm, and glides into the sea of love, vibrating. I'm cutting a wave with Anselm's scissors and plant it on Shulamit's head. She starts talking: *"Du bist Maler, Wort Gewitter Eis und Blut."*

Maybe. Maybe. "What do you see?" "I see a theory of the moon," the pianist says. "You are the crystal woman." "Who taught you to talk like that?" "You did." I sip ashes through the straw, and imagine another feedback. I'm the crystal woman. I cast my reflection on your strength and your power gets divided by four. Das ist *Melancholia* für Paul Celan, *Sol Invictus* für Jean Genet, *Konstellation* für Margarethe, und *Sternenfall* für Shulamit. You can't drown in the last straw. I make a wish for the utterance: You are powerful, my love, and I believe you.

About the Author

... actually, my favorites are tulips.

www.ingramcontent.com/pod-product-compliance
Lightning Source LLC
Chambersburg PA
CBHW022014160426
43197CB00007B/421